YOU C

EARLY AMERICAN BATTLES

AT THE BATTLE
OF THE IRONCLADS

AN INTERACTIVE BATTLEFIELD ADVENTURE

by Matt Doeden

Consultant:
Richard Bell, PhD
Associate Professor of History
University of Maryland, College Park

CAPSTONE PRESS
a capstone imprint

You Choose Books are published by Capstone Press,
1710 Roe Crest Drive, North Mankato, Minnesota 56003
www.mycapstone.com

Library of Congress Cataloging-in-Publication Data
Library of Congress Cataloging-in-Publication data is available on the Library of
Congress website.

978-1-5435-0290-9 (library binding)
978-1-5435-0294-7 (paperback)
978-1-5435-0298-5 (eBook PDF)

Editorial Credits
Adrian Vigliano, editor; Bobbie Nuytten, designer;
Kelli Lageson, media researcher; Kathy McColley, production specialist

Photo Credits
Alamy: Niday Picture Library, 10; Bridgeman Images: Private Collection/Photo
© Don Troiani, 30, 41; Getty Images: Universal History Archive, 69; Granger
Historical Picture Archive: 55; Library of Congress Prints and Photographs
Division: Cover, 25, 44; National Archives and Records Administration/WAR
AND CONFLICT: 6, 60, 64, 96; Naval History & Heritage Command: 16, 78,
88, 93, 104; North Wind Picture Archives: 50; Shutterstock: Alexey Pushkin,
Design Element, Atlantis Images, Design Element, Lukasz Szwaj, Design Element;
Wikimedia: Library of Congress's Prints and Photographs Division, 100; XNR
Productions: 35

Printed in the United States of America.
010830S18

Table of Contents

ABOUT YOUR ADVENTURE

You are living through a pivotal time in the history of the United States. The North and the South are waging a bloody Civil War. The heaviest fighting is on the ground. But the battle goes on at sea as well. Both sides are at work on secret naval weapons — ironclad ships. Can you survive this bloody time?

In this book you'll explore how the choices people made meant the difference between life and death. The events you'll experience happened to real people.

Chapter One sets the scene. Then you choose which path to read. Follow the directions at the bottom of each page. The choices you make will change your outcome. After you finish your path, go back and read the others for new perspectives and more adventures.

YOU CHOOSE the path
you take through history.

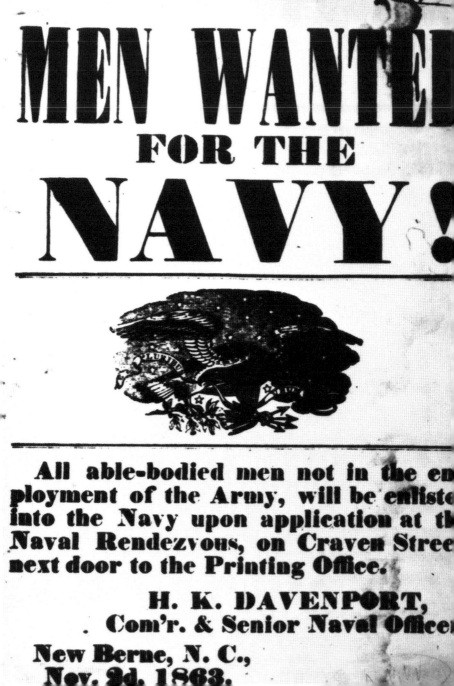

MEN WANTED

FOR THE

NAVY!

All able-bodied men not in the employment of the Army, will be enlisted into the Navy upon application at the Naval Rendezvous, on Craven Street, next door to the Printing Office.

H. K. DAVENPORT,

Com'r. & Senior Naval Officer

New Berne, N. C.,
Nov. 2d. 1863.

CHAPTER 1

THE CIVIL WAR ON THE WATER

It's March 1862 and the Civil War rages across the eastern half of the North American continent. The war is less than a year old but it is becoming clear that the fighting won't be over quickly.

On one side is the Confederacy, which is made up of 11 Southern states. Each Confederate state seceded from, or left, the United States because of disagreements over the issue of slavery. The Confederacy is now fighting to remain separate from the Union, which is made up of the remaining states.

Turn the page.

Virginia is at the heart of the fighting. That's where Union and Confederate troops meet for many of the war's early battles. The Union has a strong navy and industrial resources. The Confederacy is weak in both areas. Now the Union has moved to choke the Confederacy by blockading its ports. Union ships seek to prevent Southern ships from bringing much-needed guns and supplies to Confederate forces. The Union also tries to stop the export of Confederate crops, the lifeblood of the South's economy.

As you gaze at the Virginia sky, you wonder how long the South can hold out without supplies. You've heard whispers about each side building secret naval weapons — ships covered in armored iron plates. Will these ironclad ships even float? Could they tip the balance of power on the sea?

One way or another, the world is about to change. Forces are gathering for battle. The Battle of the Ironclads will be unlike any battle in the history of the world. It will change naval strategy forever. But will you be able to survive the events that are about to take place?

To smuggle secret Confederate naval plans north, turn to page 11.

To take command of a Southern blockade-running ship, turn to page 51.

To serve aboard a Union ship during the Battle of the Ironclads, turn to page 79.

CHAPTER 2

SECRET PLANS

You move through the mansion's bedrooms, pulling sheets off one bed after another. As you work you pay little attention to the voices that spill out of the study and down the hallway.

"This will change the war," says one voice. You recognize the speaker as your owner.

A Confederate engineer, your owner has many visitors. You are a slave with no formal education and little chance to learn what's happening in the war. This makes it difficult to understand many of the conversations you overhear. But you're smart and you can tell that this is about something really important. You stop what you're doing and listen.

Turn the page.

"How can one ship change the war?" asks a second voice.

"We're rebuilding the USS *Merrimack*," your owner answers. "It'll be called the CSS *Virginia*. We've got a team of engineers on the project. The entire hull will be ironclad. The ship will be nearly invincible. The Union domination of the seas is about to end. Just look at these plans. The Yankees will never see it coming!"

Suddenly, footsteps thunder down the hallway. In a flash you go back to gathering sheets. As your owner walks past the open door, he hesitates for a moment, staring at you. Pretending to be calm, you hum a quiet tune. He continues down the hallway without a word.

You let out a deep breath. That was close. If he had caught you eavesdropping, you would have been punished. The fact that you're a girl and a house slave might have spared you a brutal whipping. But if your owner is in the wrong mood … there's no telling what he might do.

The footsteps fade away down the stairway. You're all alone.

With a load of bedding under one arm, you take a few quiet steps toward the bedroom door. The glow of the lamp in the study warms the otherwise dark corridor.

Quietly, you creep down the hall, careful not to make a sound. As you reach the entrance of the study, your heart races. It beats so hard and so fast that you place a hand on your chest. You cannot go in. If you were caught sneaking around in the study, there would be no mercy for you.

Turn the page.

Yet you can't help yourself. You step inside, inching toward the large oak desk. On it is spread a broad sheet of paper. It shows plans for the Confederate ship — the ship that is supposed to give the South control of the seas.

If this ship will help the South win the war, I have to do everything I can to warn the Union, you tell yourself. You've overheard enough of your owner's conversations to know that the only hope you have of being free one day is for the Union to crush the Confederacy. This may be your only chance to help make that happen.

Glancing over your shoulder, you scoop up the plans and tuck them into the stack of bedding you're carrying. Trembling, you stride out of the study, down the hallway, and down the stairs. You try to act as if nothing unusual is happening.

Your owner and his guest, a Confederate officer, stand on the front porch, just outside the front door. As you come to the bottom of the stairway, your nerves get the best of you. You stumble, tripping over one of the sheets. As you collapse on the floor, the bedding spills out in front of you — feet from where the two men stand.

You wince, expecting swift punishment. But as you look up, you realize that the bedding still completely covers the stolen plans. Your owner looks down at you with annoyance.

"Get up, girl," he barks. "I want those sheets clean for our guest tonight. Go!"

Turn the page.

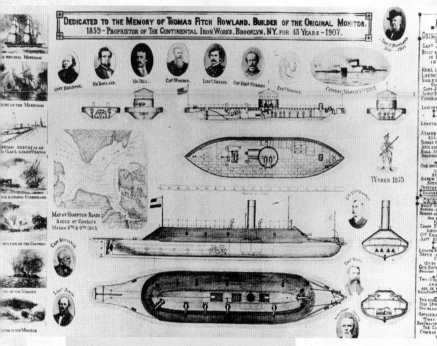

A drawing depicts the plans for two ironclad ships — the USS Monitor and CSS Virginia.

As quickly and carefully as you can, you scoop up the bedding, still certain you'll be discovered at any moment. But the men turn away. In a moment, you're out of the room and around a corner.

You slump back against a wall, desperately trying to catch your breath and calm your nerves.

What have I done? you ask yourself. Suddenly, your idea of stealing the plans and delivering them to the Union seems foolish. You are a young slave girl who has never left Virginia. What chance do you have to sneak critical military plans north? It's absurd. It's crazy.

You wonder if you could just turn around and sneak the plans back onto the desk. No one would ever have to know.

To return the plans to the study, turn to page 18.

To flee north with the plans, turn to page 21.

You can't believe the risk you took. Stealing secret war plans? Running away north? You've lived on this wheat plantation your entire life, and you've seen how slaves are punished for even minor offenses. You can't begin to imagine what would happen to you if you were caught.

"How foolish," you mutter to yourself as you turn and hurry back up the stairs.

You let the bedding slip to the floor, gather the plans, and hurry back into the office. As you rearrange the paper on the desk, you hear your owner's voice at the top of the stairs. "Let me collect a few things before we go," he says. You look up to see him standing in the doorway.

"What are you doing, girl?" he thunders. "Step away from the desk!" He grabs you roughly by the arm, pulling you toward the door. You lose your balance, stumble, and flail onto the floor.

Your owner's eyes fill with rage. He snatches you up and shoves you out the door. Your upper arm burns with pain as he drags you down the stairs and calls for the plantation's overseer.

"Ambrose!" he shouts to the overseer. "I caught her skulking about in my office. She's going to need punishment."

"Right away, sir," Ambrose says.

"No," says your owner. "Tomorrow morning. I'll deliver this punishment myself. Just get her out of the house. Now!"

Soon you are locked in a small room on the outskirts of the slave quarters. You're shaking, drenched in sweat. You've never seen your owner so angry. You sit there for hours, terrified of what will happen. Finally, late in the night, you drift off to sleep.

Turn the page.

You're awakened by a rustling sound. The door to the room opens. Instinctively, you back up against the far wall. A man steps in. You're about to scream, and then you recognize him. It's Elijah, one of the field hands.

"Elijah, what are you doing?"

"Getting you out of here," he answers. "Word is that you'll be whipped within an inch of your life. Can't let that happen. Run! There's not much time!"

Peering outside, you can see a whisper of dawn on the horizon. If you're going, you have to go now. But where will you go? What will you do? Can you leave behind the only life you've ever known?

To run, turn to page 33.

To stay and face your punishment, turn to page 36.

You're filled with doubt. How can you do this? You've never even left Virginia and now you're thinking about fleeing north with secret war plans? It's crazy, but something pulls at you. You've dreamed of a Union victory and freedom for all slaves. Now is your chance to do something about it. The risks are grave, but it's a chance you may never get again.

You hurry out of the house, down to the slave quarters, without saying a word to anyone. You collect what few belongings you have and some food, and then disappear into the night. As you leave the property, you realize that you're also leaving behind everyone you've ever known. You are completely alone for the first time in your life. What's worse, you're also a fugitive. If you're caught, it could mean your life.

Turn the page.

You travel north by night, resting and staying out of sight by day. On your second night, you hear the baying of dogs in the woods nearby. The sound paralyzes you with fear. But the sounds pass. Later, you hear the distant sound of cannon fire. You wonder if it's a battle, or just army drills.

On your third night, just before dawn, you're moving through a wooded area when you're startled by a man's voice. "Hey, you!" The voice is low and gravelly. The unexpected sound of it jolts your entire body.

To answer, go to page 23.

To flee deeper into the woods, turn to page 38.

You freeze, heart racing. The man calls out again, "Hello there, can you hear me?"

"Yes sir," you answer, your voice quavering.

"Come," he says. Your instinct is to run but something about the voice draws you in. You take a few steps in the direction of the sound. That's when you see him. It's a soldier, clad in blue. He's lying on a bed of leaves, a piece of cloth tied tightly around one of his thighs. Even in the pre-dawn darkness, you can see that his trousers are soaked in blood.

"Union?" you ask. It's the only word you can manage to get out in your fear.

The man nods. His face is covered by a patchy red beard. He appears to be in a great deal of pain.

"I'm a scout," he says. "I was shot in the leg when my unit was ambushed by rebels. I can't walk."

Turn the page.

Suddenly feeling more comfortable, you kneel down next to the man. He smells terrible — he probably hasn't bathed in months. Some of the older women at the plantation taught you a little about medicine. But you don't need to be an expert to know this man is in trouble.

"Hold still," you instruct, taking the cloth he has tied around his leg. "This tourniquet isn't tight enough. I'm going to retie it."

The soldier grimaces as you pull the cloth tight and tie the knot.

"Thank you," he whispers, just before he drifts off to sleep. You stare at him as he rests. If there are Union scouts here, then you must be getting close to Union-held territory. Your hand goes to your pack, which contains the precious plans for the Confederate ironclad. For the first time, you feel like you really might make it.

Wounded Union soldiers rest near a building after a day of fighting in Fredericksburg, Virginia.

You look north, eager to get back on the move before full daylight comes. You're so close now. But what are you to do with this man? Leave him here? Hope that he can make his way back to his unit on his own? Or stay to help, putting your own mission at risk?

You put your head in your hands and sigh.

To stay with the Union soldier, turn to page 26.

To continue north, turn to page 29.

You rest your hand on the soldier's forehead. He's burning up with fever. You don't even know this man's name but you feel you must help him.

You spend the early morning hours tending to him. You hold a cool cloth to his forehead and check his tourniquet. You're happy to see that the flow of blood from his wound seems to have stopped. Sometime around noon, he wakes. The man looks at you through crusty eyes and manages a weak smile.

"Thank you," he says, weakly extending his hand. "Private James Samuelson. I do believe you've saved my life."

By nightfall, James feels ready to move. "We can't stay here," he says, groaning as he puts weight on his injured leg. He's in great pain but he refuses to stop moving. You tell him about the plans you're carrying.

"Look, I'm just a soldier," he replies. "I don't know anything about ships or secret plans. But if you think you've got something, I'll help you deliver it north. We're in this together now."

You spend the night moving along a dirt road, since James cannot walk on the uneven ground of the woods. You track over the western bank of the Delaware River, pressing ever north toward Washington, D.C.

As you come around a bend, the crack of a rifle echoes across the landscape. Both of you stop immediately. There, in the road before you, stand half a dozen armed men.

"Militia," James whispers.

Turn the page.

The militia men are a ragtag group. Two of them appear to be in their 60s. A few look like mere teenagers. A very large man carrying an old-fashioned musket stands before them all. He fires another shot into the air.

"Well, look here," he bellows. "A Yankee! What are you doing with this man, girl?"

The six men slowly advance, drawing closer. James' hand rests on his revolver, concealed in the folds of his uniform. The militia men seem so focused on James that they don't seem to care about you right now. You wonder if they would bother following you if you made a break into the woods. It's not like you'd be much good to James in a fight. Yet the idea of abandoning him now seems horrible.

To stay with James, turn to page 31.
To make a dash for the woods, turn to page 44.

You check the tourniquet one more time. After digging in your pack, you pull out a small strip of dried beef and place it next to the man. Next, you remove your half-filled water tin, take a small sip, and leave that with him as well.

"Good luck, soldier," you whisper, then turn away and continue your journey.

You move north for another hour or so before daylight forces you into hiding. You fall asleep in a stand of bushes, well out of sight of anyone who might be looking. You stay hidden there throughout the day and then venture back out as the sun dips below the horizon.

Sometime around midnight, you see the glow of firelight in the distance. Soon, you hear voices as well. It can only be one thing, an army camp. But which army?

Turn the page.

The Union camp of the 3rd Maine and 38th New York Regiments spreads out in a rural area in 1861.

Silently, you move through the brush, closer and closer. Then you spot two men, probably sentries. They're wearing blue uniforms. It's a Union camp!

To step out and announce yourself to the sentries, turn to page 40.

To stay in hiding until morning, turn to page 42.

You don't know what these men plan to do. But you don't want to leave James — not now.

"Weapons on the ground," shouts the big man. "Now!"

Moving slowly, James lifts his revolver out before him and gently places it on the ground. With a grimace, he reaches down to his boot, pulls out a knife, and sets it next to the gun.

"I'm wounded," he calls out.

The big man laughs. It's a mean laugh that makes your skin crawl. "Hear that, men? He wants medical attention. Maybe we should just amputate that leg for him here and now."

Several of the younger men snicker. One raises a rifle, pointing it right at James.

Turn the page.

A shot rings out. You wince. But to your shock, it's the big man who crumples to the ground. You hear another shot, then another. Two of the militia men are down while the others scramble away into the woods.

Moments later, two blue-clad soldiers emerge from the trees. They're on horseback and each is carrying a rifle.

"Are you all right?" they ask. James explains the situation. He tells them about his wound and the plans you're carrying.

"Just give them to us," one of the men replies. "We'll take them back to camp with us."

To hand the plans over, turn to page 46.

To insist on carrying them to the camp yourself, turn to page 47.

What choice do you have? Staying here could mean a whipping or worse. Nervously, you step outside and wrap Elijah up in a hug. He pushes you away.

"There's no time. Here, take this." Elijah pushes a small pack into your hands. "It's not much, but it will get you well on your way. Now go!"

Your head spins as you start to move your feet down the long lane to the plantation. A slow, uncertain walk turns into a run, then a sprint. As you reach the main road and leave the plantation, the reality hits you. You're now a fugitive slave. A criminal who can be shot on sight.

You take a quick look back over your shoulder at the only home you've ever known. *No*, you tell yourself, fixing your gaze forward. *It was never my home.*

Turn the page.

You put as much distance as you can between you and the plantation while it's still dark. As dawn brightens the eastern sky, you slip away from the road into a deep wooded area. There, far from the road, you hide in heavy brush. The pack Elijah gave you is filled with bits of food. You eat a few bites, determined to make the provisions last.

As the days go on, you keep traveling every night. You steer clear of anyone who might see you and question where you're going. You continue hiding during the daytime, narrowly escaping discovery on more than one occasion. Pressing ever north, you make your way into northern Virginia, into Maryland, then on to Pennsylvania.

To reach freedom in the North, slaves often had to travel hundreds of miles across dangerous land.

You're free. You've escaped the South and your life of slavery. You don't know what life holds for you here in the North. It won't be easy. But at least it's *your* life. You wish you had been able to carry those naval plans with you. Instead, the North will have to win the war without your help.

THE END

To follow another path, turn to page 9.
To read the conclusion, turn to page 101.

You're touched by Elijah's gesture. Trying to help you was a big risk. But you can't go.

"I'm sorry, Elijah. This is my home. Everyone I know and love is here. If I leave now, I can never come back. I can never see the people I love again. No, I'll stay and face whatever is coming."

Elijah gives you a pained look but nods to show that he understands. When morning comes, Ambrose, the overseer, leads you out of the shack. "You're lucky," he says. "The master had to leave this morning on urgent war business. He left your punishment to me."

You hold your breath. Ambrose goes on.

"Now you know that I don't mind whipping slaves. But I'm talking about field slaves. Men. I don't whip women. If the lady of the house got word that I had, she'd come for my head."

"Then what will you do?" you ask, trembling.

Ambrose gives you a long, cold look. "Five days confinement. No food. And you'll be barred from the house in the future. I'm moving you to the stables. You'll be cleaning out the stalls."

Five days without food is something you can bear. But banishment from the house is a blow. You've never worked anywhere else.

As Ambrose leads you away, you can't help but wonder at your future. Should you have run off with the plans? Would it have made a difference in the war? You'll just have to hope the Union is victorious without your help.

THE END

To follow another path, turn to page 9.
To read the conclusion, turn to page 101.

Someone has spotted you! You dart away from the voice, moving through the darkness as tree branches scrape at your face and body. You run until you can't catch your breath. You just want to get away from whoever it was that called out to you. Without thinking, you charge out of the woods into an open meadow.

"Halt!" shouts a booming voice. "Not another step! Identify yourself!"

It's a Confederate soldier. As you stop and look out ahead of you, your heart sinks. You've run headlong into a Confederate camp.

"Nobody," you reply, trying to sound meek. "Just a slave girl."

"What are you doing out here, girl?" the soldier asks, stepping into view. He looks hardened and weathered. His uniform is in tatters. He points his rifle directly at you.

"I'll just turn around and go," you say.

"Not so fast!" He grabs you by the arm. As he does, your pack falls from your hands. The stolen plans spill onto the ground.

"What have we here?" the soldier asks, picking up the papers. He looks them over.

"Please, just let me go," you beg. But his grasp on your arm tightens.

"No, no, no," he laughs. "I have a feeling the general is going to want to see this. The Confederacy doesn't take kindly to spies." He lowers his voice to a cold, terrifying whisper. "Treason, you know, is punishable by death."

As he leads you away, you feel numb. You've failed and you're going to pay a terrible price.

THE END

To follow another path, turn to page 9.
To read the conclusion, turn to page 101.

You can't believe that you've made it! You joyfully step out into the open and call out.

Within seconds a rifle crack splits through the night air. You feel something push you back — hard. You stumble and fall over onto your back. It's only after you hit the ground that you feel a sharp pain in your gut. It takes a second to process what just happened. You've been shot.

The Union sentries approach you cautiously. You try to speak but can't catch your breath. Suddenly, your body feels very light. The world around you seems to grow dimmer and dimmer by the second. One of the men is talking to you but you can't seem to focus on what he's saying.

You're dying. You have just enough time to realize that before you lose consciousness. Your final thought is of the plans. You can only hope that they find them and *use* them.

The Union's 169th New York Volunteer Infantry makes camp in Virginia.

Maybe, just maybe, you've succeeded in your mission. You hope you've played a small part in helping to free those who are still enslaved.

THE END

To follow another path, turn to page 9.
To read the conclusion, turn to page 101.

You stay low, out of sight. This is what you've come for, but stepping out of the darkness into an army camp seems unwise. So you wait.

Once the sun has climbed up over the horizon, it's time to move. You gather your things and step out into the clearing.

As you approach the camp, you raise your hands, showing that you are unarmed. It doesn't take long before you're spotted. Half a dozen soldiers converge on you outside the camp. They shout at you and order you not to move.

Finally, a man approaches you. He introduces himself as Franklin, a Union captain. "What's your business?" he asks.

You tell him everything about your former owner, his position in the Confederacy, the secret plans, and your journey north. The captain appears skeptical until you show him the plans. He stares at them for several moments and then returns his gaze to you.

"If these are real, you've done a great service to the United States of America," he says. "We're marching north today. You'll join us. Let's get you into free territory, where you'll be safe. We need to deliver these plans to Washington, D.C., as soon as possible."

The captain extends his hand. You reach out and shake it — as a free woman.

THE END

To follow another path, turn to page 9.
To read the conclusion, turn to page 101.

If you stay here, you'll almost certainly be captured. You can't hesitate. "Good luck, James," you whisper. Then you dart off the road and sprint toward a nearby stand of trees.

The 8th New York state militia make camp in Arlington, Virginia, in June 1861. Both the North and the South relied heavily on militia groups early in the Civil War.

You run as fast as you can. But the distant crack of gunfire tells you all you need to know. The militia men may be more interested in capturing a Union soldier. But they're not about to let a fugitive slave escape into the wilderness.

The shot slams into your back. You're thrown forward, landing in a heap. For just a moment, you imagine that it's not that bad. You try to get back up but all your strength seems to be gone.

As the world fades around you, you realize the truth. You've been shot squarely in the back. You try to cry out but you can't catch your breath. The plans lie in the pack beneath your body. And that's where they'll stay. You've failed in your mission and it has cost you your life.

THE END

To follow another path, turn to page 9.
To read the conclusion, turn to page 101.

You've done your part. You feel like a weight has been lifted off your shoulders as you hand over the plans.

"We'll make sure they get to Washington, D.C.," says one of the Union officers. "Get along now. We'll take this man back to camp with us. He'll get the treatment he needs."

The men help James onto one of the horses. "Take care of yourself," James calls out as they ride off. "Thank you for everything."

And just like that, you're alone. The militia men have scattered but there's no telling whether they'll be back.

You fix your gaze north and keep marching. You won't stop until you reach free territory.

THE END

To follow another path, turn to page 9.
To read the conclusion, turn to page 101.

"I'd like to carry the plans to the camp myself," you answer. "I want to come north. I need your help."

One of the officers, who introduces himself as Lieutenant Lambert, nods. "I suppose that's fair. Come on, let's go."

The officers help James onto one of the horses, while you climb on the other with the lieutenant. A few hours later, you ride into a massive Union Army camp. James is taken to the field hospital, while Lambert leads you through mazes of tents to the heart of the camp. There, a short, stocky general stands before a large map set on a table. When Lambert introduces you, the general looks skeptical.

Turn the page.

You unfold the plans and lay them out on the table. The general peers intently at the plans.

"Yes, yes, yes," he mutters, mostly to himself. Finally, he looks up and addresses you. "The Union has been working on a similar ship," he says. "I expect our friends in the navy will be most interested to see what you've got here. Perhaps it's time we accelerate the timetable for our own ironclad."

He reaches out a rough, scarred hand. "Your country thanks you for your service. I'm told that you wish to come north to start a new life. We'll make sure you get north safely."

"Will this really matter in the war?" you ask.

The general shrugs. "Who knows? It just might. You took a terrible risk in bringing us these plans. I can promise we'll do all we can to use them to our advantage."

Lambert arranges for you to travel north with a small garrison. As you ride out of the camp on horseback, you realize that a new chapter of your life is beginning. You can't wait to see where it takes you.

THE END

To follow another path, turn to page 9.
To read the conclusion, turn to page 101.

CHAPTER 3

BLOCKADE RUNNER

Waves batter your ship as a spring storm passes over the Atlantic Ocean. A lightning bolt streaks across the sky with a booming crack of thunder coming only seconds behind it.

You're not worried. You've been a sailor your entire life and you've been through storms far worse than this one.

The young woman steering the ship beside you isn't so confident. At first you were surprised when Hazel asked to serve on your crew. You couldn't imagine a well-mannered Southern lady accepting a rough life on your ship.

Turn the page.

But you've learned that Hazel is no Southern belle. She's as tough as any man on your crew and works twice as hard.

"It's just a squall," you assure her. "The wind will blow, the waves will rise, but it will all pass quickly enough." In the month since Hazel came on board, you've never seen her afraid. But this storm has her nervous.

Though small compared to large naval vessels, your ship is fast and sturdy. Counting yourself and Hazel, it has a crew of just four people. The other two, an old sailor named Abner and a freed slave, Ezekiel, are below decks playing cards.

Sure enough, the storm blows past quickly. Hazel's expression relaxes as the winds die down and the thunder fades away.

The sea is black, without moonlight or starlight. That's perfect for your mission. The Union has blockaded Southern ports up and down the Atlantic Coast. The northern strategy is to use the blockades to smother the Confederacy by denying them crucial supplies. The blockades also prevent the South from exporting the all-important cotton crop.

You gaze to the west. Somewhere out there, a dozen miles or so, lies the coastline of Virginia. The coast is heavily guarded by the Union Navy. It's time to head in.

To smuggle weapons into Virginia for the Confederate war effort, turn to page 54.

To smuggle cotton out of Virginia to sell in the Caribbean, turn to page 56.

"Well, are we going in, sir?" Abner asks. "We've got a fortune in weapons here. The army needs them and we need to get paid. What are we waiting for?"

Abner is anxious. But you're cautious. The Union has been stepping up its patrols. Just last month, an old friend of yours was captured for running weapons. You can't be too careful.

"Let's move in slowly," you say. As Hazel steers the ship toward shore, you use a small telescope to keep your eyes on the shoreline. You squint, spotting a glint of light inland. Then another followed by another.

You don't want to wait out here any longer than you have to. Every moment you're on open water is a moment you could be spotted.

A Confederate blockade runner is hit by Union ships as it passes near Charleston harbor in South Carolina.

But you're not sure about what you're seeing on the shoreline either. "Hazel," you shout, preparing to give her an order.

To order her to turn the ship around, turn to page 62.

To tell her to put into shore to unload your cargo, turn to page 73.

The South's economy is built on cotton. A major reason for the Union blockade is to prevent the Southern states from exporting this important crop. By selling it abroad, the South can bring in much-needed funds to support the war effort.

You turn over navigation to Hazel. She knows these waters well. Under the cover of night, you move toward shore, keeping a sharp eye out for Union ships. Hazel steers the boat into a small bay, where your cargo will be waiting.

Ezekiel raises a lantern, then opens and closes it three times. On shore, the answer comes. A light flashes back at you — once, twice, three times.

"It's clear," Ezekiel calls. Hazel begins to take the ship in.

Two men meet you as you drop anchor just offshore. They begin loading bales of cotton. Your cargo hold is about half full when you hear gunshots coming from a wooded area just inland. The sharp bangs are followed by an eerie silence. Even the frogs have stopped croaking.

"Trouble!" Abner calls.

"We're not full," Hazel answers. "Those gunshots could have been anything. We should wait until our cargo bay is full."

They look at you, waiting for a decision.

To flee to the open sea, turn to page 58.

To wait until the ship is full, turn to page 61.

"I've got a bad feeling," you say, staring into the darkness. "Anchors up!" You hate to leave with less than a full load but it's more important to avoid getting caught.

Abner and Ezekiel spring into action, bringing up the anchor and setting sail to deeper waters. As you move away from the small cove, the sound of more gunfire carries out across the water.

"Union troops," Abner hisses, spitting into the water. "That could have been a disaster."

You've gotten away, but are still nervous. If the Union had troops on the ground, it's possible that there are still some navy ships out here, ready to spring a trap. But as the minutes tick by, you start to breathe easier.

As the excitement fades, the crew fall back into their routines. Hazel, sharp-eyed and reliable, steers the ship by night. You take the wheel by day. Abner and Ezekiel keep the ship in good working shape and help you navigate.

Your destination is Havana, Cuba. The port is loaded with ships that can carry your cargo to England to sell. You push south, tracing the Atlantic coast toward Florida.

The weather grows hot and humid as you push south. You find yourself daydreaming as your ship bobs over the waves. Suddenly, Ezekiel's voice raises up. "Ships closing to starboard!"

In a moment, all four of you are up. Sure enough, three ships appear on the horizon. "Union ships," Abner says, peering through a telescope. "They're closing fast."

Turn the page.

A crew member stands next to a large cannon on the deck of a Union ship.

You open your sails, trying to outrun the ships. But no matter what you do, the ships just creep closer and closer.

"Dump the cargo," Ezekiel suggests. "It's weighing us down."

"No!" Hazel protests. "We can't dump it. It's the whole reason we're here!"

Abner looks at you, awaiting your decision.

To dump the cargo, turn to page 69.

To keep the cargo and hope for more favorable winds, turn to page 71.

You stare at the shore. Seeing no movement, you nod to Hazel. "Keep loading, but let's do this quickly."

The minutes tick by. Your heart races. Something about this doesn't feel right. You're about to order Abner to pull up the anchor when more shots ring out. You can hear a bullet whiz past your ear. Another shot blows a hole in the hull of the ship.

"Freeze!" shouts a voice. A dozen blue-uniformed soldiers step out of the cover of the woods, each with a rifle pointed directly at you.

To dive into the water and abandon your ship, turn to page 65.

To try to escape with your cargo, turn to page 67.

Your instincts scream at you to turn around. You learned long ago not to ignore them. "Turn it around!" you order. "Get us as far from shore as you can!" There's no way of knowing if you've made the right decision, but it's better to be cautious. Losing a day is a lot better than losing your ship — or your life.

As your ship bobs up and down on the ocean waves, you stand on the deck. Hazel, Abner, and Ezekiel are all getting some much-needed rest while you stand guard. You watch as the eastern horizon slowly brightens, then as the sun finally peeks over the horizon.

Just as you're about to head below decks, a noise echoes across the ocean. It's like thunder but much sharper — and the sky is clear. BOOM! There it is again. You hear the rustle of feet as your crew rushes to see what's happening.

"Bring it in a little," you order. Abner takes the helm, guiding the ship closer to shore. Through a small telescope, you scan the horizon.

"There!" you shout, pointing. "Warships ahead. They're ours!"

You can barely believe what you're seeing. Several wooden-hulled steamers are flanked by a ship unlike anything you've ever seen. The ship appears to be clad in armor.

The armored ship blasts its guns at a pair of Union blockade ships. Another series of loud booms thunders across the ocean. Something explodes. The fireball is big enough that the others can see it without the telescope.

Turn the page.

An ironclad ship is well protected by heavy metal plates and cannons.

"If there's a battle, the Union ships will be distracted," Ezekiel points out. "Might be a good time to put in with our cargo."

"In broad daylight?" Hazel asks, bewildered.

"If not now, then when?" Ezekiel replies.

To try delivering your cargo while the battle plays out, turn to page 75.

To stay here and watch the battle, turn to page 77.

The Union soldiers don't wait for an answer. They start shooting. Hazel gasps as a shot hits Abner in the shoulder, spinning him around.

Your ship has been caught, but you're not going to be captured so easily. You take a deep breath and dive into the dark water. The bitter cold takes your breath away, but you dive deeper. Even under the water, you can hear the muffled sound of gunfire above.

You're a skilled swimmer and you kick for all you're worth. You stay underwater as long as you can, until it feels like your lungs are about to explode. Coming up for air, you look around you. As you look at your ship, you gasp. It's on fire! The flames crawl across the deck. Once they hit the cotton in the cargo bay, the ship goes up like a torch.

Turn the page.

With another deep breath, you dive and swim. You keep swimming for what seems like hours, covering as much distance as you can. Finally, you come ashore in a small cove.

You're cold, alone, and you have no idea if your shipmates are alive or dead. You slump down onto the rocky beach and sob. How did it all go so wrong? And what will you do now that your ship has been destroyed?

You always knew that blockade running was dangerous business. You gambled, and you lost.

THE END

To follow another path, turn to page 9.
To read the conclusion, turn to page 101.

"Anchors up!" you shout. Abner and Ezekiel pull up the anchor as Hazel tries to pilot the ship safely out to sea.

Rifle fire rains down on the ship. You can hear bullets peppering the hull.

But somehow, no one is hit. After a few minutes of pure terror, you're safely miles out to sea.

"We made it," Hazel sighs.

But the celebration doesn't last long. The shots have punched holes in the hull — some of them below the water line. "We're taking on water," Abner tells you.

Stepping below decks, you survey the damage. The situation is dire. Water is pouring in through several holes in the hull. "We can't bail it out," Abner says. "It's coming in too fast."

"How long do we have?" you ask.

Turn the page.

Abner shakes his head. "Minutes. It's over, sir."

The four of you rush above decks and lower the ship's rowboat into the water.

"Oh no," Hazel says.

You see it too. Several holes are blasted in the rowboat too. It won't float.

The four of you stand, taking in your fate. Your ship is sinking. There's no rowboat. And help is not on the way.

The water rushing into your ship is very cold and very dark. And in a matter of minutes it's going to swallow up the ship, leaving you with little hope of survival.

THE END

To follow another path, turn to page 9.
To read the conclusion, turn to page 101.

You sigh. Abner is right. Those ships are closing in. If you're caught, the Union will seize the cotton and destroy your ship.

"We have no choice," you say. "We must dump the cargo."

Hazel steers the ship as you, Abner, and Ezekiel undertake the backbreaking work of unloading bale after bale of cotton. One after another, you dump them overboard, until the cargo bay sits empty.

Turn the page.

Crews in the Bahamas work quickly to unload bales of cottom from Confederate ships.

"It's working!" Hazel calls. With no cargo, the ship is lighter and faster. The Union ships begin to fade in the distance. By nightfall, they've disappeared.

Hazel is upset. You sit beside her on the deck as Abner turns the ship around. "It's part of the job," you say. "We know the risks and losing some cargo isn't nearly as bad as the alternative. They would have destroyed our ship, Hazel. We'd be done. At least this way, we can try again."

And that's what you'll do. You're not a soldier or a naval sailor. But you love the excitement of blockade running despite the danger. You're determined to keep going as long as your ship keeps floating.

THE END

To follow another path, turn to page 9.
To read the conclusion, turn to page 101.

You can't bear the idea of dumping your cargo. "No, we've come so far and risked so much. Dumping our cargo now would be like giving up. Maintain our course. There's still a chance we can catch a wind and outrun them."

Over the next hour, you watch nervously as the Union ships close in. They're steamboats — not reliant on the wind. Eventually you realize that you have no hope of outrunning them.

As soon as the ships are within range, the Union sailors fire warning shots. When you don't stop, they fire again. But this time, it's not a warning. Your ship is hit near the stern and you begin to take on water.

"What do we do, captain?" Ezekiel asks, panic growing in his voice. You don't have an answer.

Turn the page.

"They're going to board us," Abner says. "The captain and I will be taken prisoner. I don't know what they'll do with Hazel. Ezekiel, you tell those sailors that you're a slave and that you had no choice. That might save you."

You run your hand along your ship, feeling the rough wood grain beneath your fingers. It's so strange to think that in a matter of hours, the ship will be at the bottom of the ocean. You've failed, and you can't stop asking yourself, *where did it all go wrong?*

THE END

To follow another path, turn to page 9.
To read the conclusion, turn to page 101.

"Take us in," you tell her. If every glint of light scares you away, you've picked the wrong job.

The ship glides in toward shore. You know this shoreline so well that you don't even need moonlight to visualize every curve and bend. Hazel steers the ship toward a small cove. There, you can signal your contact and unload the cargo. The Confederacy will have a new stash of weapons and you'll be on to your next smuggling run.

The ship slips around a bend and in toward shore. Here, the sea is calm. It's sheltered from ocean breezes. Normally, you can hear croaking frogs and chirping crickets as you draw near. But tonight, everything is silent. All you hear is the water as it breaks beneath the ship's bow.

"Something's not right," you call to Abner, who is preparing to drop anchor. "This doesn't feel like —"

Turn the page.

BOOM! A sound like thunder shatters the silence. A moment later, the ship jerks, as if you've run aground. *BOOM*! Another blast. This time you see the flash of light that comes with it. Cannon fire! You throw yourself to the deck, covering your head as debris rains down on you.

Out of the corner of your eye, you see Ezekiel diving into the water. Hazel is close behind. Abner lies on the port side, clutching his ribs. He's calling out to you, but you can't hear anything over the ringing in your ears.

Another shell hits. It rips into the cargo bay, igniting some of the gunpowder stored there. In an instant, the ship explodes in a ball of flame.

You hope Ezekiel and Hazel got far enough away to survive the blast. You're not so lucky.

THE END

To follow another path, turn to page 9.
To read the conclusion, turn to page 101.

"Ezekiel is right," you say. "Hazel, take us in."

The crew scrambles as you head to shore. To your north, the blasts continue. Occasional glances through your telescope show you that the strange iron ship appears almost unstoppable. It cuts down the wooden-hulled Union ships in its path, leaving them in ruin.

Ezekiel's instincts are correct. With the Union Navy engaged in battle, the blockade patrols are nonexistent. It feels strange to pull into your secret cove in broad daylight but you don't see another soul.

Your contact on shore is Charles, an old man with a wooden leg. He owns the land here and uses it as a secret port for small blockade-runners. Charles hobbles out to greet you as you pull in.

"What's happening out there?" Abner calls.

Turn the page.

Charles excitedly describes the battle as you unload your cargo. "It's the CSS *Virginia*," he huffs. "It's been fitted with iron armor. The Union ships can't so much as scrape it. This could be it," he continues, clapping you on the back. "This could be the ship that finally breaks the Union blockade."

Even as the others celebrate the thought, you find yourself unable to share their excitement. One ship won't be enough to tilt the balance of naval power in this war. The Union is still far better equipped and you'd be shocked if they didn't have a similar ship of their own. Yet any Confederate success on the sea is a good thing. You've delivered your cargo, which will soon be in the hands of Southern soldiers. You've done your part and you'll continue to do it, as long as you're needed.

THE END

To follow another path, turn to page 9.
To read the conclusion, turn to page 101.

"Hold position," you order, keeping your eyes on the distant battle. You stay there through the day, watching as the armored Confederate ship tears through the wooden-hulled Union ships. Morning turns into afternoon, then into evening.

By the next morning, more Union ships have arrived. "Now we can't go in to deliver our cargo," Hazel says coldly. "We missed our chance."

"Take us south," you order. "We'll find somewhere else to put in."

You give the order with confidence. But you wonder if the crew still trusts your decisions. After this voyage it might be time to step away. You just don't seem to have the stomach for this business anymore. One way or the other, your time as a blockade runner is over.

THE END

To follow another path, turn to page 9.
To read the conclusion, turn to page 101.

CHAPTER 4

BATTLE ON THE SEA

The boom of cannon fire rumbles over the Atlantic Ocean. Your ears ring and you're barely able to hear your shipmates shouting all around you.

Your ship, the USS *Minnesota*, is stationed off the port of Newport News, Virginia. It's the flagship of the Union's Atlantic Blockading Squadron, charged with blockading the Southern port.

"Enemy vessels incoming! The *Congress* and the *Cumberland* are under attack!" shouts one of the officers on the main deck.

Turn the page.

Far across the water you look to see three Confederate ships rounding a peninsula called Sewell's Point. They've come to try to break the Union's blockade of the Southern port. Two of the incoming ships appear to be ordinary wooden-hulled steamers. It's the third ship that holds your gaze. The beast of a ship sits low in the water. It's loaded with guns, as well as a ram in front. But what sets it apart is its hull. From prow to stern, the ship is covered in iron plates.

You've heard of the Union's own "ironclad" ship, but you've never seen it. Now, looking out over the waters of the Atlantic, you can barely believe your eyes.

"How can that thing even float?" The question comes from Seaman Adams, a young sailor who only recently joined the *Minnesota*'s crew.

Before anyone can answer, the sound of cannon fire once again rumbles over the water.

"Slip the cables!" shouts the ship's captain, G.J. Van Brunt, running his hand across his forehead and through his hair. As the *Minnesota* breaks free of the cables that anchor it in place, the captain orders it straight toward the enemy ships. Over the water, you can see the Confederate ships advancing. The great ironclad — the CSS *Virginia* — bears down on the wooden frigate USS *Cumberland*. It rams into the smaller ship. You gasp as the *Cumberland* is shredded to pieces.

"No!" shouts Adams. You remain silent but your gaze is locked on the battle that you're about to join. You know a lot of the men on the *Cumberland*. You can only hope they survive.

Turn the page.

As the *Minnesota* gains speed, the battle unfolds. The *Cumberland* is destroyed. The USS *Congress* is forced to surrender. Smaller ships and tugs scatter before the advancing Confederate force.

Suddenly, the hull of the *Minnesota* quivers. The entire ship lurches.

"We've run aground!" calls a voice.

You look out. Smoke rises up above the destroyed *Cumberland*. Out of the smoke comes the ironclad *Virginia*. It's bearing down straight on the *Minnesota*.

To use one of the *Minnesota's* guns, go to page 83.

To go to the bridge, turn to page 84.

The *Virginia*, weighed down by its iron armor, moves slowly. Several other ships flank it. The *Minnesota* is well armed and you take your station as a gunner. As Adams loads the gun, you take aim and fire. The shell explodes from the barrel of the gun in a high arc but splashes into the water far short of the *Virginia*.

The battle is on. Both ships exchange fire. The *Virginia* remains well out of range. Meanwhile, the CSS *Patrick Henry*, a wooden frigate, draws closer.

"What about that one?" Adams asks, pointing at the smaller *Patrick Henry*. The *Virginia* is the main threat, but with its iron armor even a hit might not do much damage. You look from the hulking *Virginia* back to the *Patrick Henry*, which is just on the edge of your range.

To fire on the *Patrick Henry*, turn to page 85.

To save your ammunition to engage the *Virginia*, turn to page 92.

You join Captain Van Brunt as several Confederate ships engage the *Minnesota*. With the ship grounded, there's little to do but order the men to fire on any Confederate ship within range. The *Minnesota* has several successes, including a direct hit to the CSS *Patrick Henry*, but the *Virginia* continues to lurk in the distance.

"Why aren't they engaging, Captain?" you ask.

Van Brunt shakes his head. He looks very tired but he never stops to rest. "They're waiting," he responds. "We're at low tide right now and with all that iron, the ship has a deep draft. They don't want to ground themselves the way we have."

"So we wait?" you ask.

The captain sighs and nods. "We wait. Unless I misjudge my enemy, the *Virginia* will come for us at dawn. Be ready."

Turn to page 87.

Adams is right. Firing on the *Virginia* seems pointless. Instead, you target the *Patrick Henry*. This time, your shot is on the mark. The blast tears through the ship's hull. You watch as a cloud of smoke and steam rises above the ship. A cheer goes up from your fellow sailors on the deck of the *Minnesota*.

"Nice shot!" Adams yells.

Disabling the Patrick Henry is a small victory, however. You've still got the *Virginia* to contend with and it's bearing down on the *Minnesota*.

As the sun begins to set in the western sky, the *Virginia* fires at the *Minnesota* but the shots fall well short of their mark.

"Why are they staying so far back?" Adams asks in one of the quieter moments.

Turn the page.

"They're afraid of coming closer," answers a voice from behind you. You turn to see Captain Van Brunt. "They know we're stuck here and can't move until the tide comes in. They'll come for us again at dawn."

With that the captain moves on, taking stock of the damage to the *Minnesota*. Sure enough, he's right. At sunset the fighting stops. An uneasy calm settles in over the water.

Go to page 87.

It's a long, somber night. With the sun down, a glow from the burning *Congress* flickers over the ocean. You can't sleep, so you remain on deck with Adams at your side. The *Minnesota* is quiet. You and Adams stand near one of the ship's lifeboats, near the stern. Sometime after midnight, the *Congress* explodes in a great ball of fire. The sound of it shatters the silence.

"How could this happen?" Adams asks. You've been wondering the same thing. The Union's superiority on the seas has been unquestioned throughout the war. Now suddenly, the South has this monster of a ship. You seem helpless to stop it. The *Virginia* will come again in the morning, and there's nothing you can do to change that.

Turn the page.

A damaged gun from CSS **Virginia** shows the powerful weaponry that was on board during battle.

Adams runs a hand along the lifeboat.

"You know," he whispers. "We could leave now. We'd be gone before anyone noticed."

"And become deserters?" you reply. "We'd be criminals. We'd be on the run for the rest of our lives."

"Better on the run than under the ocean," Adams says coldly.

To stay and fight, go to page 89.

To attempt to escape aboard a lifeboat, turn to page 93.

You shake your head. "I know you're afraid. So I'll pretend you didn't mean that."

Adams backs away. He clears his throat and croaks, "No, no. Of course not. I'm just thinking. That's all. I'd never desert."

You know Adams is right about one thing. Without help, the *Minnesota* stands no chance of surviving the battle tomorrow. As you stand thinking about this, a new ship steams onto the scene. It's the USS *Monitor* — the Union's version of an ironclad. The *Monitor* steams to a halt between the *Minnesota* and the *Virginia*. The *Minnesota*'s deck fills as sailors come to see the sight. The *Monitor* is no work of art. One sailor jokes that it looks like a giant iron cheesebox. But since it floats between you and certain defeat, the *Monitor* is a beautiful sight to your eyes. You can only imagine what the enemy must be thinking.

Turn the page.

Fog still hangs thick when the sun rises. After what seems like hours, the fog lifts and fighting resumes. Cheers rise up on the *Minnesota* as the *Monitor* opens fire on the *Virginia*. For the next several hours, the two iron ships exchange fire but neither is able to damage the other.

The *Virginia* turns its guns on the *Minnesota*. The Confederate ironclad peppers your wooden ship with volley after volley. "Return fire!" shouts Captain Van Brunt.

Suddenly, the *Minnesota* quivers. You're sure it's a direct hit. You whirl around to see the damage. The shot has blown a hole in the hull, near where the kegs of gunpowder are stored.

"Fire! Fire!" comes the call. The powder has ignited and it's burning inside the ship.

To rush to put out the fire, go to page 91.

To return fire on the *Virginia*, turn to page 95.

Visions of the burning *Congress* flash through your mind. There are few thoughts more terrifying to a sailor than a fire aboard ship. You rush to help put out the fire, while others remain above deck to continue the battle.

Smoke pours out of the boatswain's room. You pull your uniform up over your face to filter out the smoke. Sailors pass buckets of water down, though it does little good. One of the first to respond, you're also one of the closest to the actual fire. The heat that radiates out singes the hairs on your arms.

As you throw water on the fire, you grow lightheaded. The smoke fills your lungs, and you double over coughing.

To keep fighting the fire, turn to page 97.
To get away from the smoke, turn to page 98.

"Just load it!" you shout to Adams over the cannon fire. All around you, crew members scurry around the deck, bringing ammunition to the gunners. With the ship grounded, you're sitting ducks. It seems your only chance is to bring down the *Virginia* and force the other ships to retreat. As the battle rages around you, you wait for your shot at the Confederate ironclad.

You never get the chance. A blast comes from one of the smaller Confederate ships. The shell rips into the hull of the *Minnesota*, just below your gun. One moment, you're standing over the gun. The next, you're flying backward through the air as shards of the wooden hull rain down.

The fight will go on. But you won't be a part of it. Your story has come to a disastrous end.

THE END

To follow another path, turn to page 9.
To read the conclusion, turn to page 101.

You can't get the sight of the burning *Congress* out of your mind. How many sailors died today at the hands of the Confederate ironclad? How many more will die tomorrow? And will you be one of them?

"Alright," you agree. "Let's do it."

"We'll have to gather some things," Adams says.

You cut him off. "No. We do it now. We may not get another chance."

Turn the page.

The CSS **Virginia** fired at and destroyed the USS **Congress** on March 8, 1862.

Together, as quietly as possible, you lower the lifeboat down into the water. Adams climbs down first. Just as you're about to climb down yourself, a voice rings out.

"Halt! Identify yourselves!"

You freeze, paralyzed by indecision. An officer grabs you by the arm. He draws a pistol and aims it at Adams. "Deserters! I should shoot you both on the spot!"

He doesn't shoot you. But he does drag you to the brig. As he slams your cell door shut, you realize your mistake. Desertion is punishable by death. You wanted to survive the battle. But you know that you won't survive this.

THE END

To follow another path, turn to page 9.
To read the conclusion, turn to page 101.

Your place is on the deck. You stay at your station as others rush to deal with the fire. You fire several more shots but by this point the *Minnesota* has become an afterthought. All eyes are on the two iron ships, which blast away at each other with everything they have. You and the rest of the crew on the *Minnesota* are left to watch. Many of the crew gather on the deck, looking out at the scene.

"Can you believe that?" asks William Brown. Brown's dark skin sets him apart from most of the other sailors on the ship. He's part of an all-black crew stationed at one of the ship's forward guns.

You shake your head in amazement. Yet as the battle continues, it becomes clear that neither of the iron ships is capable of harming the other. Eventually, the *Virginia* draws away.

Turn the page.

A group of men inspect dents and other damage on the **Monitor**.

A cheer goes up on the deck of the *Minnesota*. The Confederate forces were determined to sink your ship and they failed. The blockade will remain in place. But it came at a terrible cost. The Union Navy has suffered heavy losses.

You shake your head. All that fighting and nobody won the battle. It seems like such a waste.

THE END

To follow another path, turn to page 9.
To read the conclusion, turn to page 101.

Hot air singes your eyebrows and smoke fills your lungs but you refuse to stop. As the buckets are passed down, you hurl water onto the dwindling fire. Your quick action has paid off — the fire is contained.

As you reach for yet another bucket, your body is racked with a fit of coughs. The world before you goes hazy and your vision flickers. Your chest is burning and suddenly your legs give way.

You fall hard. You're unconscious by the time your fellow sailors drag you out. And you never regain consciousness. You pushed your body too far. It was a heroic death, but your part in the Civil War has come to an end.

THE END

To follow another path, turn to page 9.
To read the conclusion, turn to page 101.

You can't breathe. The fits of coughing grow worse and worse. As quickly as you can, you rush out of danger and above decks, trying to breathe in fresh ocean air. A few minutes later, word comes that the fire has been put out.

By that time, you're on your knees. You've inhaled too much smoke and you still can't draw a full breath.

"Medic!" shouts a fellow sailor. You're conscious just long enough to see a young medic rush to your side.

You regain consciousness half an hour later. Adams stands at your bedside. "I thought we might lose you," he confesses. "The medic wants you to rest."

"The battle," you croak. Your throat feels raw.

"It's over," Adams tells you. "The *Virginia* drew off. I guess both of those iron ships just gave up on trying to damage each other."

Later, Captain Van Brunt pays you a visit. "You've done well, sailor," he tells you. "As soon as we've got this ship off this mud bar, we'll get you to a proper hospital. And don't be surprised if a promotion happens to come your way."

The Battle of Hampton Roads is over. Both sides claim victory but in truth, neither side won. The Union suffered heavy losses, while the Confederacy failed to break the Union blockade. Still, it was a battle unlike any other in naval history and you're proud to have played your part.

THE END

To follow another path, turn to page 9.
To read the conclusion, turn to page 101.

CHAPTER 5

THE BATTLE OF HAMPTON ROADS

Most of the Civil War's major battles were fought on land. The Union's naval superiority was largely unchallenged. The South didn't have the ships to wage a major naval campaign.

The most famous Civil War naval battle by far was the Battle of Hampton Roads, also known as the Battle of the Ironclads. In 1861 the Confederate government salvaged the burned and sunken USS *Merrimack*. After discovering that the *Merrimack*'s engines and machinery were undamaged, the Confederates began rebuilding the ship.

They rebuilt the ship as the ironclad CSS *Virginia*. On March 8, 1862, the *Virginia* joined other Southern ships in attacking the Union's blockade forces. They attacked the Union near a natural harbor called Hampton Roads, close to present-day Norfolk, Virginia.

The Confederate ships were largely unchallenged on that first day of fighting. Union forces had never seen anything like the *Virginia*, which seemed impenetrable with its armor of iron plates. The *Virginia* led an attack that destroyed the USS *Congress* and USS *Cumberland*. Then it turned its sights on the USS *Minnesota*, which had run aground trying to respond to the attack.

With the low tide, the *Virginia* couldn't get close enough to finish off the *Minnesota* before dark. The Southern ships retreated to deeper waters, planning to finish the job in the morning.

Left to itself, the *Minnesota* would have been doomed. But the Union had built its own ironclad, the USS *Monitor*. The *Monitor* rushed to Hampton Roads in the dark of night. "All on board the *Minnesota* felt we had a friend that would stand by us in our hour of trial," wrote the *Minnesota*'s Captain Van Brunt.

The Confederate ships returned on the morning of March 9. The acting captain of the *Virginia* saw the *Monitor* but didn't immediately recognize it as a Union ironclad. As a result the two iron ships drew close to each other. They blasted shells at each other for hours but neither could do serious damage to the other.

The USS **Monitor** sank during a storm off Cape Hatteras, North Carolina, on December 31, 1862.

The battle ended when a blast struck the *Monitor*'s pilot house, temporarily blinding its captain. The *Monitor* drew back. The acting captain of the *Virginia*, believing that the *Monitor* was in retreat, backed off as well.

Confusion reigned after the battle. Both sides claimed victory. Military historians, however, believe that neither side gained much advantage. The Union's losses were much greater but the blockade remained in place.

The battle is memorable because it marked the beginning of a new era in naval warfare. Neither of the ironclads fought in another battle and both were destroyed that same year. Yet both sides were soon hard at work building more ironclads. The days of the wooden-hulled warship were at an end.

TIMELINE

April 12, 1861—The Civil War begins when Confederate forces fire on the Union-held Fort Sumter in Charleston Harbor, South Carolina

April 20, 1861—Confederates from Virginia take over the Norfolk Navy Yard after Union forces retreat. They discover that the USS *Merrimack* has been burned and sunk but that much of its hull and machinery are intact

July 4, 1861—The U.S. Congress receives a report with information about the Confederacy's work to construct an ironclad ship. Congress begins to discuss the possibility of building a Union ironclad

January 30, 1862—The USS *Monitor* is launched

February 1862—Former slave Mary Louvestre steals secret plans for a Confederate ironclad and delivers them to Washington, D.C.

February 17, 1862—The CSS *Virginia* is commissioned. The armored ship is built from the burned remains of the USS *Merrimack*

March 8, 1862—The Battle of Hampton Roads begins when the CSS *Virginia* and other Confederate ships destroy the USS *Cumberland* and the USS *Congress*. The USS *Minnesota* runs aground while attempting to respond

March 9, 1862—The USS *Monitor* arrives to protect the USS *Minnesota*. The *Monitor* and the *Virginia* exchange fire for several hours but neither ship is able to damage the other. Both ships draw away and the battle ends

May 9, 1862—As Confederate forces abandon Richmond, Virginia, the CSS *Virginia* is destroyed to prevent it from falling into Union hands

December 31, 1862—The USS *Monitor* experiences high winds and waves. It takes on water and sinks, killing 16 crew members

April 9, 1865—The Civil War effectively ends as Confederate General Robert E. Lee surrenders to Union General Ulysses S. Grant in Appomattox Court House, Virginia

OTHER PATHS TO EXPLORE

In this book, you've seen how events from the past look different from three points of view. Perspectives on history are as varied as the people who lived it. Seeing history from many points of view is an important part of understanding it. Here are ideas for other Civil War points of view to explore.

+ Many Union sailors aboard the *Congress* and *Cumberland* were killed in the battle. Others were captured. If you had a choice, would you rather have been captured or killed? State your reasons.

+ Wooden-hulled ships stood little chance against the ironclads. Yet they attacked them anyway. Would that be a hard decision to make as a ship's captain? Why or why not? Would you attack, knowing it likely meant your death?

READ MORE

Burgan, Michael. *Spies of the Civil War: An Interactive Espionage Adventure*. North Mankato, Minn.: Capstone Press, 2015.

George, Enzo. *The Civil War*. New York: Cavendish Square Publishing, 2015.

Otfinoski, Steven. *Yankees and Rebels: Stories of U.S. Civil War Leaders*. North Mankato, Minn.: Capstone Press, 2015.

INTERNET SITES

Use FactHound to find Internet sites related to this book.

Visit *www.facthound.com*

Just type in 9781543502909 and go.

GLOSSARY

blockade (blok-AYD)—a military effort to keep goods from entering and leaving a region

Confederate (kuhn-FE-der-uht)—a person who supported the South during the Civil War

deserter (di-ZURT-ur)—a military member who leaves duty without permission

ironclad (EYE-urn-clahd)—a ship covered in armor plates

militia (muh-LISH-uh)—a group of volunteer citizens who are organized to fight, but who are not professional soldiers

mission (MISH-uhn)—a military task

plantation (plan-TAY-shuhn)—a large farm where crops such as cotton and sugarcane are grown; before 1865, plantations were run by slave labor

rebel (REB-uhl)—someone who fights against a government or the people in charge of something; a nickname for Confederate soldiers during the Civil War

Union (YOON-yuhn)—the Northern states that fought against the Southern states in the Civil War

Yankee (YANG-kee)—a nickname for Union soldiers during the Civil War

BIBLIOGRAPHY

Holzer, Harold, and Tim Mulligan, eds. *The Battle of Hampton Roads: New Perspectives on the USS* Monitor *and* CSS Virginia. New York: Fordham University Press, 2006.

Symonds, Craig L. *Decision at Sea: Five Naval Battles that Shaped American History.* New York: Oxford University Press, 2005.

Tucker, Spencer C., ed. *The Civil War Naval Encyclopedia.* Santa Barbara, Calif.: ABC-CLIO, 2011.

Ward, Geoffrey C., with Ric Burns and Ken Burns. *The Civil War: An Illustrated History.* New York: Knopf, 2009.

Weigley, Russell Frank. *A Great Civil War: A Military and Political History, 1861–1865.* Bloomington, Ind.: Indiana University Press, 2000.

INDEX